GIFTED & TALENTED®

*To develop
your child's gifts
and talents*

DINOSAURS

A Science Workbook for Ages 6–8

Written by Martha Cheney
Cover and poster illustrations by Jim Auckland
Interior illustrations by Jim Auckland and Martha Collins

**McGraw-Hill
Children's Publishing**

Columbus, Ohio

Reviewed and endorsed by Q. L. Pearce, author of more than 60 science titles, including The Dinosaur Almanac *and* The Science Almanac for Kids.

McGraw-Hill
Children's Publishing

A Division of The McGraw-Hill Companies

Send all inquiries to:
McGraw-Hill Children's Publishing
8787 Orion Place
Columbus, Ohio 43240-4027

ISBN 0-7373-0054-X

Printed in China.

1 2 3 4 5 6 7 8 9 10 STR 06 05 04 03 02

GIFTED & TALENTED® WORKBOOKS will help develop your child's natural talents and gifts by providing activities to enhance critical and creative thinking skills. These skills of logic and reasoning teach children **how** to think. They are precisely the skills emphasized by teachers of gifted and talented children.

Thinking skills are the skills needed to be able to learn anything at any time. Unlike events, words, and teaching methods, thinking skills never change. If a child has a grasp of how to think, school success and even success in life will become more assured. In addition, the child will become self-confident as he or she approaches new tasks with the ability to think them through and discover solutions.

GIFTED & TALENTED® WORKBOOKS present these skills in a unique way, combining the basic subject areas of reading, language arts, math, and science with thinking skills. The top of each page is labeled to indicate the specific thinking skill being developed. Here are some of the skills you will find:

- Comprehension—the ability to understand concepts put into sentences

- Creative Thinking—the ability to generate unique ideas; to compare and contrast the same elements in different situations; to discover imaginative solutions to problems

- Deduction—the ability to reach a logical conclusion by interpreting clues

- Inference—the ability to reach logical conclusions from given or assumed evidence

- Understanding Relationships—the ability to understand how objects, shapes, and words are similar or dissimilar; to classify and categorize

Each book in this series contains activities that challenge children. The activities vary in range from easier to more difficult. You may need to work with your child on many of the pages, especially with the child who is a nonreader. However, even a nonreader can master thinking skills, and the sooner your child learns how to think, the better.

Read the directions to your child and, if necessary, explain them. Note that the words printed in bold face are listed in the glossary at the back of the book for your reference. There is also a pronunciation guide at the back of the book. The activities should be done consecutively, as the activity on each page builds upon the skills and information presented on the pages that precede it. When your child's interest wanes, stop. A page or two at a time may be enough, as the child should have fun while learning.

The included poster is an extra learning tool that you and your child can use together. Hang the poster in a very visible place. Then whenever you get the chance, talk about the various items pictured on the poster. Ask your child questions about the poster. What additional information can he or she tell you about the picture?

It is important to remember that these activities are designed to teach your child **how to think,** not how to find the right answer. Teachers of gifted children are never surprised when a child discovers a new "right" answer. For example, a child may be asked to choose the object that doesn't belong in this group: a table, a chair, a book, a desk. The best answer is **book,** since all the others are furniture. But a child could respond that all of them belong because they all could be found in an office. The best way to react to this type of response is to praise the child and gently point out that there is another answer, too. While creativity should be encouraged, your child must look for the best and most **suitable** answer.

GIFTED & TALENTED® WORKBOOKS have been written and endorsed by educators. This series will benefit any child who demonstrates curiosity, imagination, a sense of fun and wonder about the world, and a desire to learn. These books will open your child's mind to new experiences and help fulfill his or her true potential.

Many people are fascinated by dinosaurs. What do you think the world was like when dinosaurs lived on Earth?

Describe what is happening in this picture. Then color it any way you like.

You have probably heard some amazing stories about dinosaurs, but no one has ever seen a real, live dinosaur. That is because dinosaurs lived many millions of years before there were any people. How do we know that dinosaurs ever lived on Earth? We have some important clues. These clues are called **fossils**.

Different kinds of fossils form from plants and animals that died a long time ago. When leaves, shells, or bones get buried in mud, they can leave an **impression,** or outline, in the mud. This outline can turn into rock as time passes, forming one kind of fossil.

Can you tell what made each of these fossils? Write the answer under each picture.

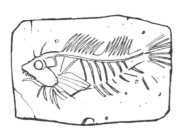

_____   _____

_____   _____

Here is a way to see what fossils look like. Ask an adult to help you do this project.

You will need these supplies:
- modeling clay
- small, shallow plastic container, such as a margarine tub
- shell, small bone, or leaf
- nonstick cooking spray
- plaster of paris

1. Press a ¾-inch-deep layer of modeling clay into the container. Make it as flat and smooth as you can.

2. Press a shell, bone, or leaf into the clay to make an impression, then remove it.

3. Spray the clay with a little nonstick cooking spray.

4. Mix the plaster of paris according to the directions on the package. Pour a ¾-inch-deep layer of plaster on top of the clay.

5. When the plaster is completely dry, remove the clay and plaster from the container. Carefully peel the modeling clay away from the plaster to see how it looks.

Before the 1800s, people who found dinosaur bones and teeth did not know what they were. Little by little, people realized that these fossils were different from those of any other group of animals. These animals were somewhat like lizards, a type of reptile, but were generally much bigger. They decided to call this group Dinosauria. The name *dinosaur* comes from this word, which means "terrible lizards."

Why do you think "terrible lizards" was chosen for the name? What do you think people knew about dinosaurs at this time?

_____

_____

_____

Paleontologists are the scientists who study fossils. Over the years, these scientists have been able to learn a lot about dinosaurs and other animals that lived a long time ago.

Why do you think paleontologists and other people continue to look for fossils today?

_____

_____

Paleontologists look for fossils all over the world. When they find fossils they want to study, they must carefully dig them out of the ground. The bones are wrapped in plaster so they won't break. Then they are sent to a laboratory, where they are carefully unwrapped. Paleontologists study the fossils to find out what type of animal they belonged to and when it lived.

Sometimes paleontologists find parts of a dinosaur's **skeleton**. The skeleton can be put together and shown in a museum.

These pictures show some of the jobs paleontologists do. Number the pictures in order to show when each job should be done.

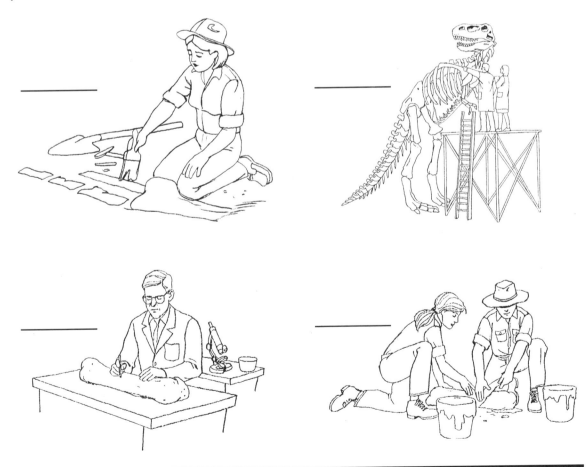

Here is a picture of a dinosaur called Brachiosaurus. Below it is a picture of its skeleton. The bones of a skeleton help give an animal's body its shape. Do you see how this dinosaur and its skeleton look alike?

Have you ever seen a dinosaur skeleton in a museum? If you have, what did you notice about it?_____

_____

_____

Draw a line from each dinosaur to the picture of its skeleton.

Iguanodon

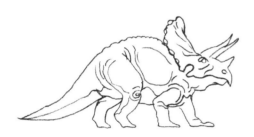

Triceratops

Stegosaurus

Some fossils show what a dinosaur's skin looked like. From these fossils we know that some dinosaurs had bumpy, leathery skin. Others had **scales** or bony **plates** covering parts of their body. These fossils do not show what colors a dinosaur's skin was, so there is no way for us to know.

What do you think it would feel like to touch each of these dinosaurs?

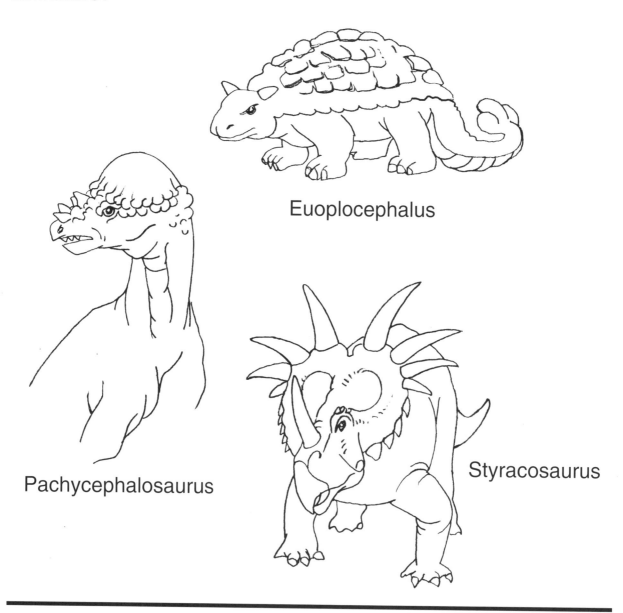

Euoplocephalus

Pachycephalosaurus

Styracosaurus

Some people think that the dinosaurs were green and brown. These colors would have helped them hide in the plants and trees. Other people think the dinosaurs were very colorful, like some birds and lizards are today. Bright colors sometimes help an animal attract a **mate**.

Here is a picture of two dinosaurs. What colors do you think these dinosaurs were? Color the picture below any way you like.

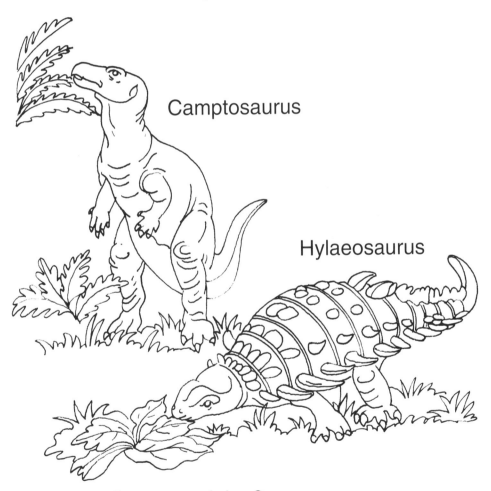

Camptosaurus

Hylaeosaurus

What are these dinosaurs doing? _____

_____

_____

There were two main groups of dinosaurs: Saurischians, or lizard-hipped dinosaurs, and Ornithischians, or bird-hipped dinosaurs.

Dinosaurs of all sizes could be found in each group, but the lizard-hipped dinosaurs included some of the biggest dinosaurs that ever lived. The hipbones of the Saurischians looked like the hipbones of lizards today. Many of these dinosaurs had sharp claws on their feet. Certain lizard-hipped dinosaurs were meat-eaters, while others were plant-eaters.

All bird-hipped dinosaurs were plant-eaters. These dinosaurs usually had beak-shaped mouths and hooflike claws on their toes. The hipbones of Ornithischians looked like the hipbones of birds today.

Draw a circle around each lizard-hipped dinosaur below and on the next page. Draw a square around each bird-hipped dinosaur.

Ankylosaurus

Deinonychus

Tyrannosaurus

Protoceratops

How do you know which group each of these dinosaurs belongs
to? _____

_____

Some dinosaurs were incredibly big, while others were small.

The pictures below and on the next page should give you an idea of how big, or small, some dinosaurs were.

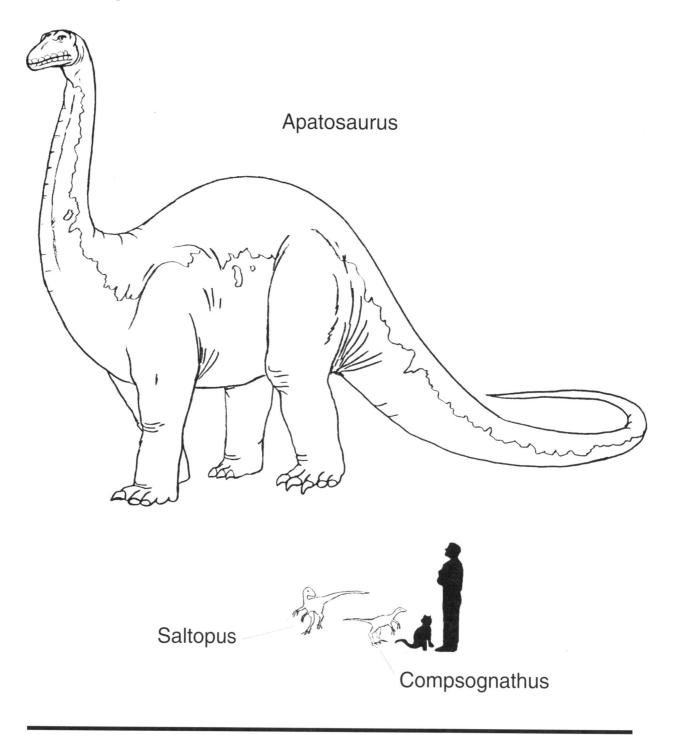

Apatosaurus

Saltopus

Compsognathus

Stegosaurus

Hadrosaurus

Which of the dinosaurs on these pages were smaller than you are? _____

_____

Can you think of something that is about the size of a Stegosaurus? _____

Can you think of anything that is bigger than an Apatosaurus?

_____

17

Plant-eating dinosaurs and other animals are called **herbivores**. These dinosaurs had flat teeth for grinding the plants they ate. Sometimes they had teeth for cutting and snipping off twigs and branches as well.

This dinosaur, a Triceratops, was an herbivore. Draw some food on the page for the Triceratops to eat.

Do you think plants have changed since the time of the dinosaurs? Why or why not?_____

_____

Animals that eat meat are called **carnivores**. Dinosaurs that were carnivores had very sharp teeth. Some of the teeth had jagged edges to help them cut up their food. The Tyrannosaurus rex was a carnivore. It had 60 very sharp teeth that were each 3 to 6 inches long.

Color the picture any way you like.

What do you think this Tyrannosaurus rex would like to eat?

_____

Which of the two dinosaur **skulls** shown below do you think belongs to a meat-eater? Circle your answer.

How do you know? _____

How else can you tell the difference between a carnivore and an herbivore? _____

What do you think the dinosaur below ate? _____

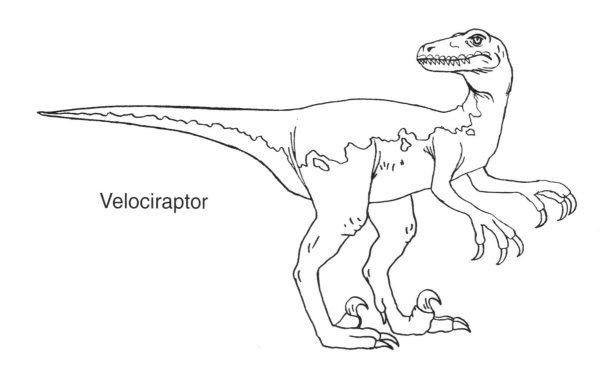

Velociraptor

Circle the dinosaurs below that you think were meat-eaters. Put a square around the plant-eaters.

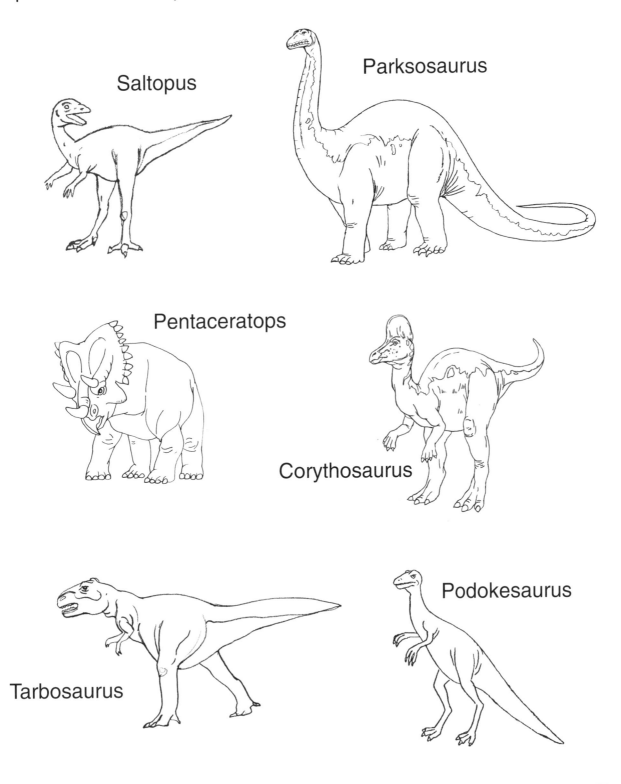

Saltopus

Parksosaurus

Pentaceratops

Corythosaurus

Tarbosaurus

Podokesaurus

This Tarbosaurus is looking for food. What is Psittacosaurus doing? What do you think will happen next?

Color the picture below, then write a story on the next page about this picture.

Plant-eating dinosaurs did not use their teeth or claws to **defend** themselves against the meat-eaters. They had other ways to defend themselves. Some dinosaurs had sharp horns on their faces, and some had a hard bony collar , called a frill, to protect their necks.

Color the frill on this dinosaur red. Color the horns blue.

Triceratops

Some dinosaurs were covered with tough, thick plates or pointed spikes . Some of these dinosaurs even had strong tails, which they could use like a whip or a club.

Ankylosaurus

Why do you think the plant-eaters had this type of **armor,** but the meat-eaters did not? _____

_____

What kind of armor do you think worked best? Make up your own dinosaur by adding pieces of armor to the picture below. Explain how this armor would help protect the dinosaur you've created.

Some dinosaurs protected themselves by running away from other dinosaurs. Running fast also helped some carnivores catch slow-moving dinosaurs. Paleontologists figure out the speed of certain dinosaurs by measuring the distance between their tracks and studying the length of their legs. Therefore, dinosaurs with long legs could probably run faster than dinosaurs with short legs.

This graph shows how fast some dinosaurs may have been able to run. Use the graph to answer the questions below.

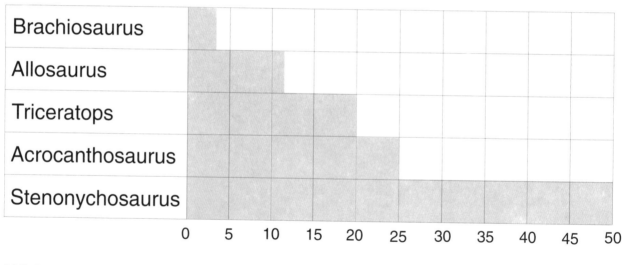

Miles Per Hour

Which dinosaurs on the graph could run faster than Allosaurus?

_____

Which dinosaur could run faster, Acrocanthosaurus or Triceratops? _____

Which dinosaur could run faster than any other dinosaur on the graph? _____

What was another way some dinosaurs, such as this Sauropod, protected themselves and their young from meat-eating dinosaurs?

Cross out the letters that spell the name of each of these pictures to find out.

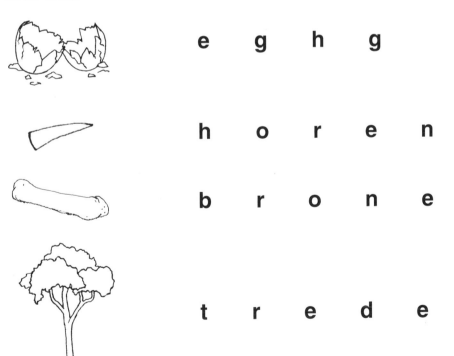

e   g   h   g

h   o   r   e   n

b   r   o   n   e

t   r   e   d   e

What word do the remaining letters spell? ___ ___ ___ ___

Some dinosaurs protected themselves by herding together. Fossil tracks show that when certain dinosaurs traveled, or moved, in a group, they kept the young dinosaurs in the center.

Why would this be a good way for some dinosaurs to protect their young? _____

_____

Color the picture any way you like.

Pachycephalosaurus had a thick bone on the top of its head. Knobs and spikes stuck out from this dome and the dinosaur's nose. Pachycephalosaurus may have crashed heads with rival dinosaurs to become the leader of the herd or to win mates.

Circle the two pictures below that are exactly alike.

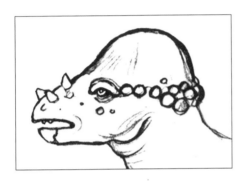

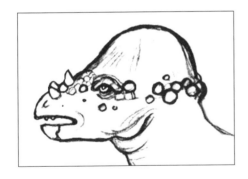
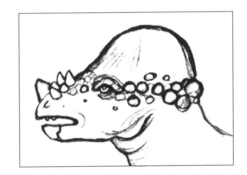

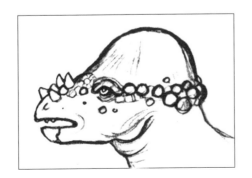

Paleontologists believe that most dinosaurs **hatched** from eggs. They have found many different kinds of dinosaur egg fossils. The biggest eggs found have been about 10 inches long, but many eggs are much smaller.

What do you think a baby dinosaur looked like before it hatched from an egg? Draw any type of baby dinosaur you want inside this egg.

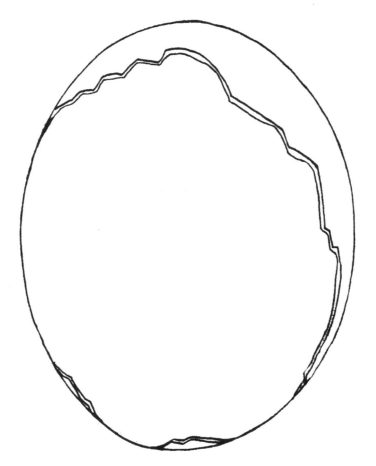

Most dinosaurs looked very much like their parents when they were born, but some features, such as horns and frills, took time to develop. This is what an adult Protoceratops looked like.

Number the pictures in order to show how a Protoceratops grew.

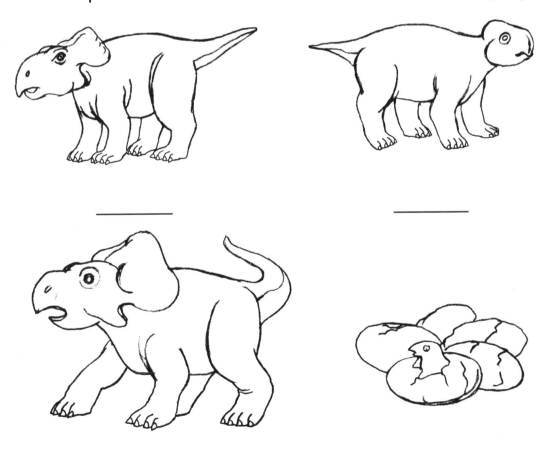

Paleontologists believe that some dinosaurs took very good care of their babies after they hatched, unlike many reptiles today. In Montana, the bones of more than a dozen baby dinosaurs were found in and around a large round nest. It was 7 feet across. The remains of an adult dinosaur were also found near the nest. This dinosaur was named Maiasaura. The teeth of the baby dinosaurs were worn, showing that they had been eating plants. Perhaps the mother Maiasaura brought the plants to the nest for the babies to eat.

Color the picture any way you like.

Use the information on page 32 to complete each sentence below.

This Maiasaura nest was found in ◯◯ __ __ __ __ __.

The remains of the adult were near a large __ ◯ __ __ .

The nest was ◯ __ __ __ __ in shape.

The __ __ __ __ ◯ of the baby dinosaurs were worn because they had been eating __ __ __ __ ◯ __.

Unscramble the letters in the circles to find the meaning of the name Maiasaura.

"Good __ __ __ __ __ __ lizard"

Think of some animals living today that care for their young until they are grown. What are some of the things these animals do to care for the baby animals?

Diplodocus was one of the longest dinosaurs. It was 85 to 100 feet long! Diplodocus had a very long neck and a small head. Its tail was about 45 feet long! Diplodocus probably swayed its tail back and forth to keep other dinosaurs away.

Connect the letters in alphabetical order to make a picture of Diplodocus.

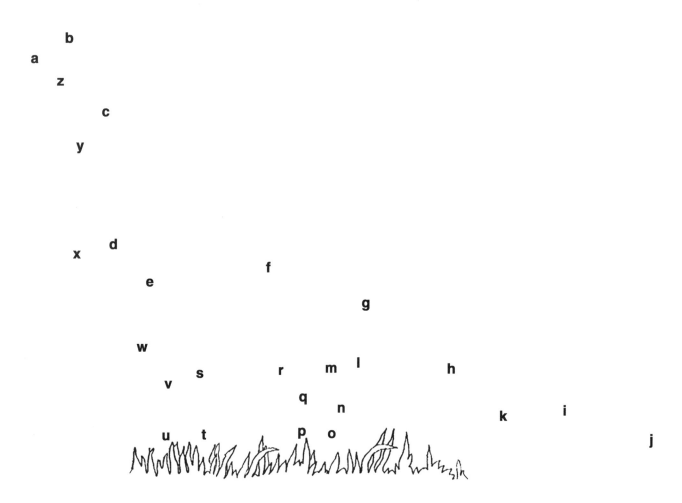

Stenonychosaurus was a very fast and smart dinosaur. In fact, some scientists think it was the most intelligent of all the dinosaurs. It had sharp claws and could see well, so it was probably a good hunter. Many paleontologists think this dinosaur is the same as the one called Troödon.

Carefully copy the lines in each numbered box into the square on the grid below that has the same number.

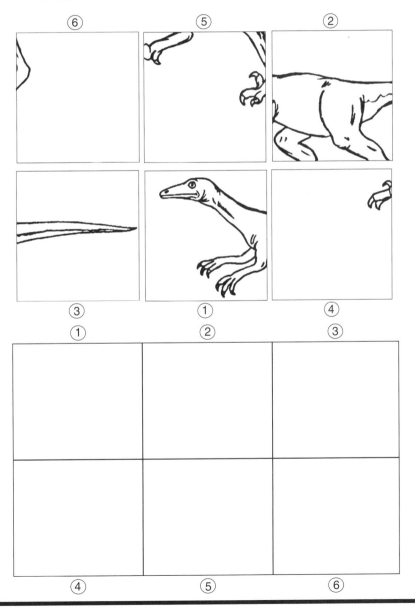

Gallimimus looked sort of like a giant ostrich. It had long, thin legs and could run fast. Its hands were not very strong. Gallimimus had a long neck and a small head. It had jaws that looked like a beak. Gallimimus did not have teeth. It probably ate eggs, plants, and fruit.

Fill in the blanks, then use your answers to complete the crossword puzzle.

Across

3. Gallimimus probably ate plants and __ __ __ __.
4. It did not have __ __ __ __ __.
6. Its __ __ __ __ __ were weak.

Down

1. Gallimimus had jaws that looked like a __ __ __ __.
2. Gallimimus looked somewhat like a giant __ __ __ __ __ __ __.
5. It could __ __ __ fast.
7. It had a __ __ __ __ __ head.

Velociraptor was a meat-eating dinosaur. It was only about 6 feet tall. Velociraptor had sharp claws on its hands and feet. One claw on each foot was like a long, slashing knife. Velociraptor could run fast. Its name means "speedy thief."

Why do you think this dinosaur was called "speedy thief"?

_____

How many different words can you make using the letters in the name Velociraptor?

VELOCIRAPTOR

_____   _____

_____   _____

_____   _____

Stegosaurus had large bony plates on its neck, back, and tail. Scientists are not sure why the dinosaur had these plates. Perhaps the plates protected Stegosaurus, or maybe they helped it warm up and cool down.

Stegosaurus was about 25 feet long and weighed over 3 tons. It had a very small head and brain. Stegosaurus walked with its head close to the ground because its front legs were shorter than its back legs. Stegosaurus had sharp spikes on the end of its tail.

Color the Stegosaurus plates purple. Color the spikes red. Color the rest of the dinosaur any way you like.

Use the information on page 38 to complete each sentence below.

Stegosaurus had a small __ __ ◯ __.

Stegosaurus had sharp __ ◯ __ __ __ __ on the end of its tail.

Stegosaurus was about 25 __ __ __ ◯ long.

Stegosaurus weighed over 3 __ __ __ ◯.

Stegosaurus had bony __ ◯ __ __ __ __ on its back.

Its head was close to the __ __ __ __ ◯ __.

Unscramble the letters in the circles to find out what Stegosaurus liked to eat.

Stegosaurus ate __ __ __ __ __ __.

Pentaceratops was one of the dinosaurs that had a lot of armor. It had a horn above each eye and one on its nose. It also had something that looked like a horn on each cheek. Pentaceratops had a very large frill. Its body was about 20 feet long. Pentaceratops was a plant-eater.

Complete the picture by drawing the missing half of this Pentaceratops.

Camarasaurus was a fairly large four-footed plant-eater. It had a long neck and a very strong but short tail.

Carefully copy the lines in each numbered box into the square on the grid that has the same number.

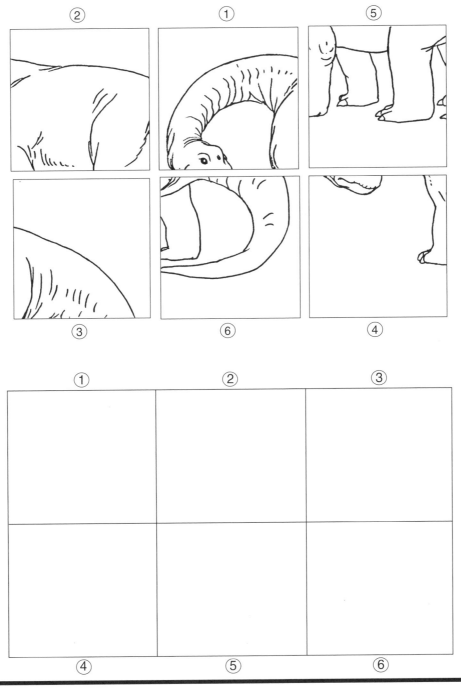

Apatosaurus was a very large dinosaur that walked on four feet. It was about 70 feet long! It had a long neck, which allowed it to munch on leaves from tall trees. It also had a long tail. This dinosaur had very strong bones to support its weight. Apatosaurus was covered with tough, leathery skin.

Create a rhyme about Apatosaurus. Fill in each blank below using the information given above.

Its neck was long.
Its bones were __ __ __ __ __ __.

It reached with ease
To the tops of __ __ __ __ __.

Its skin was __ __ __ __ __.
And that's enough!

Ankylosaurus was about 35 feet long and weighed about 5 tons. It had a short neck and stubby legs. The body of Ankylosaurus was covered with thick, leathery skin and bony plates. It also had rows of knobs and spikes on its body. Ankylosaurus had a tail that ended in a big bony club, which could be used to fight off other dinosaurs. The dinosaur used its small teeth and jaws to eat plants near the ground.

Ankylosaurus weighed __ __ __ __ __ __ __ __.
                1 2 3 4   5 6 7 8

Ankylosaurus had a __ __ __ __ __ neck.
               8 9 6 10 5

Ankylosaurus had bony plates, __ __ __ __ __ __, and knobs for armor.
                         8 11 2 12 4 8

Ankylosaurus ate __ __ __ __ __ __.
              11 13 14 7 5 8

Use the answers above to find the letter that goes with each number. Fill in the blanks to find a nickname for Ankylosaurus.

__ __ __ __ __ __ __ __ __   __ __ __ __
10 4 11 5 2 13 2 14 7   5 14 7 12

Why is this a good nickname for Ankylosaurus?

43

Ingenia was a small dinosaur. It weighed about 60 pounds and was less than 5 feet long. It probably ate insects and the eggs of other dinosaurs.

This Ingenia is looking for food. Color the path that it must take to get to its food.

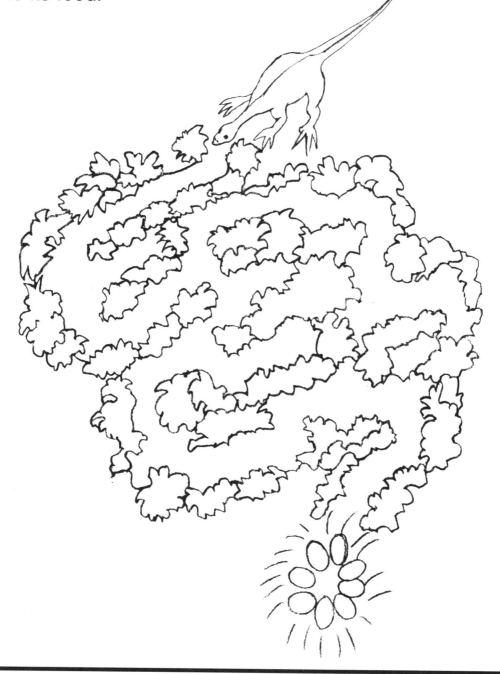

Compsognathus was a tiny dinosaur that was no bigger than a chicken! Because it weighed about 5 pounds, Compsognathus was probably quick and light on its feet. It could chase down insects and other small animals, then use its sharp teeth and claws.

There are six of these tiny dinosaurs hiding in the picture below. Can you find them all? Circle each one.

Coelophysis was a small, slender dinosaur that weighed only about 60 or 70 pounds. This little dinosaur was a meat-eater, and it had sharp teeth and a long jaw. It was also a fast runner. Coelophysis lived in **herds,** or family groups.

Connect the letters in alphabetical order to find a picture of Coelophysis.

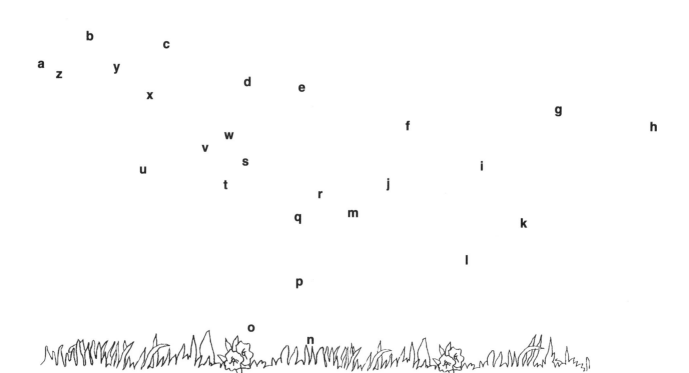

Dacentrurus was a fairly small dinosaur. It was only 15 feet long, and it weighed about 1 ton. It had two rows of spikes on its back and tail. Dacentrurus walked on all four feet. It was a plant-eater.

How many different words can you make using the letters in the name Dacentrurus?

DACENTRURUS

_____   _____

_____   _____

_____   _____

Now use each of these words in a sentence.

Saltasaurus was a large dinosaur that walked on four feet. It had a fairly long neck and a long, thick tail. Saltasaurus was almost 40 feet long from nose to tail. Saltasaurus had tough plates, studs, and tiny spikes covering its back.

Ask an adult to help you cut a piece of string that is 40 feet long. Take the string outside and lay it out in a straight line on the sidewalk.

Was Saltasaurus bigger than a car? _____

Can you think of something that is as big as Saltasaurus was?

_____

Can you name an animal living today that has hard plates covering part of its body? _____

Corythosaurus was fairly large. It was about 30 feet long and weighed more than 2 tons. It had bumpy skin and a hollow, rounded crest covering its head. Corythosaurus was a plant-eater, and it had many rows of teeth for grinding food. Scientists think it ate pine needles and leaves. Corythosaurus probably ran on two feet with its tail out for balance.

Corythosaurus was fairly large in __ __ __ __.
1 2 3 4

In fact, it was about __ __ __ __ __ __   __ __ __ __ long.
5 6 2 7 5 8   9 4 4 5

Corythosaurus had a large crest on its __ __ __ __.
6 4 10 11

Its skin was __ __ __ __ __.
12 13 14 15 8

It probably ate __ __ __ __ __ __.
16 4 10 17 4 1

Use the answers above to find the letter that goes with each number. Fill in the blanks to find the meaning of this dinosaur's name.

__ __ __ __ __ __   __ __ __ __ __ __
6 4 16 14 4 5   16 2 3 10 7 11

Do you think this is a good name for Corythosaurus? Why?

Dilophosaurus was about 20 feet long. It walked on two feet. It had strong legs and short arms, and its fingers and toes had sharp claws. Dilophosaurus was a meat-eater, and it had large jaws lined with sharp teeth. It had two bony crests along the top of its head. Paleontologists are not sure why Dilophosaurus had these crests. Can you think of a reason why?

Complete the picture by drawing the missing half of this Dilophosaurus.

Parasaurolophus had a long crest on the top of its head. This crest was about 5 feet long! Some paleontologists think that the tube helped the dinosaur smell. Others believe that the tube gave Parasaurolophus a loud voice.

Look at each Parasaurolophus shown below. Circle the two pictures that are exactly alike.

What is different about each of the other pictures?

Pteranodon lived around the same time as the dinosaurs, but it was not a dinosaur. Pteranodon had leathery wings and was more than 25 feet across from one end of a wing to the other. While it is likely that Pteranodon could fly, it was probably better at gliding. Pteranodon most likely flew over water, then dived down to catch fish to eat.

Color the picture below, then write a story about Pteranodon on the next page. Describe what you think the Pteranodon might have seen as it glided through the air.

Plesiosaurus was about 10 feet long. It was not a dinosaur, but it did live during the same time period. Plesiosaurus lived in the sea, and it had flippers to help it move through the water. Plesiosaurus used its long neck to search for fish and other small animals in the sea.

Fill in the blanks, then use your answers to complete the crossword puzzle.

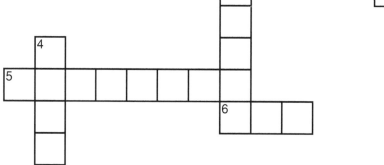

Across

1. Scientists learned about Plesiosaurus by studying __ __ __ __ __ __ remains.
3. Plesiosaur was about __ __ __ feet long.
5. Plesiosaur was not a __ __ __ __ __ __ __ __.
6. It lived in the __ __ __.

Down

1. Plesiosaurus had __ __ __ __ __ __ __ __ instead of legs.
2. It had a __ __ __ __ neck.
4. It ate __ __ __ __.

What's wrong with this picture? Find the parts of the picture that don't make sense and circle them.

What if dinosaurs were alive today? Wouldn't it be exciting to have a dinosaur for a pet? What problems do you think it might cause?

Color the picture any way you like. Then write a story about having a pet dinosaur on the lines on the next page.

These dinosaurs would probably not have lived in the same place at the same time. Do you remember the names of these dinosaurs? Say them out loud. Then color the picture any way you like.

What happened to the dinosaurs? About 65 million years ago, all the dinosaurs died out. Perhaps the weather changed over time, making summers too hot and winters too cold for the dinosaurs. Or maybe an **asteroid** hit the earth, sending up clouds of dust that blocked the sun and destroyed many kinds of plants and animals, including the dinosaurs.

No one knows for sure why the dinosaurs died out. But after surviving for 150 million years or more, the dinosaurs were gone. Can you think of some reasons why the dinosaurs disappeared? Write your answers on the lines below.

_____

_____

_____

_____

_____

_____

_____

_____

_____

_____

_____

Glossary

armor—The protective covering on the body of an animal.

asteroid—A small planet, or celestial body, that orbits a sun; nearly all asteroids are rocky.

carnivores—Animals that eat other animals; also called meat-eaters.

defend—To protect against danger or an attack.

fossils—Remnants, impressions, or traces of organisms of the past that have been preserved as rock in the Earth's crust.

hatched—Emerged from an egg when ready to be born.

herbivores—Animals that eat plants; also called plant-eaters.

herds—Numbers of animals of one kind that live or travel together.

impression—A form or shape that can occur when one object touches another.

mate—Either member of a pair of animals that can produce babies together.

paleontologists—Scientists who study fossil remains to learn about the Earth and its inhabitants of long ago.

plates—Pieces of armor, or protective covering, on an animal's body usually made of bone.

scales—Small, flattened, hard, and clearly marked sections that form part of an animal's external body covering.

skeleton—The strong protective structure that supports an animal's body. It may be inside or outside the body.

skulls—The hard, bony structure inside the heads of animals that have an internal skeleton. The skull encloses and protects the brain and chief sense organs and supports the jaws.

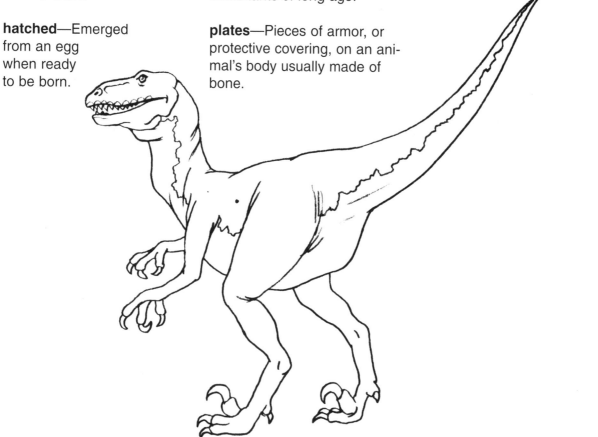

Answers

Page 5
Answers will vary.

Page 6
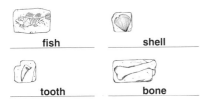

fish   shell

tooth   bone

Page 8
Sample answer: They believed that dinosaurs were a huge and powerful relative of the modern lizard.
Sample answer: They hope to discover new fossils that will help them learn more about dinosaurs and what Earth was like when they lived.

Page 9
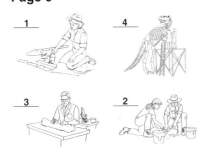

1   4

3   2

Page 10
Sample answer: It was very big.

Page 11
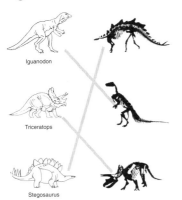

Iguanodon

Triceratops

Stegosaurus

Page 12
Answers will vary.

Page 13
Sample answer: They are eating.

Pages 14–15
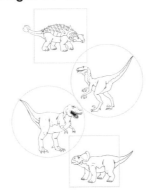

Sample answer: By looking at their feet and mouths.

Pages 16–17
Compsognathus and Saltopus were smaller than a child.
A school bus might be about the size of a Stegosaurus.
An ocean liner is bigger than an Apatosaurus.

Page 18
Parent: Child should draw plants.
Yes, plants have changed a lot since the time of the dinosaurs.
Rest of answer will vary.

Page 19
Sample answer: It would like to eat other dinosaurs.

Page 20

Sample answer: This skull has very sharp teeth.

Carnivores usually have claws. Herbivores usually do not have long, sharp claws.
It ate meat.

Page 21
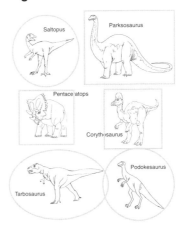

Saltopus

Parksosaurus

Pentaceratops

Corythosaurus

Tarbosaurus

Podokesaurus

Pages 22–23
Answers will vary.
Parent: You may need to help your child write the story.

Page 24
Parent: Check child's work.
Sample answer: Plant-eaters often had horns and spikes for protection because they did not have sharp teeth or claws, unlike most meat-eaters.

Page 25
Answers will vary.

Page 26
Triceratops, Acrocanthosaurus, and Stenonychosaurus could have outrun Allosaurus.
Acrocanthosaurus was faster than Triceratops.
Stenonychosaurus was the fastest of all.

Page 27
herd

Page 28
The dinosaurs' babies were smaller, slower, and weaker than them, and therefore would have been easier to kill. By herding together, the adults could protect the young dinosaurs.

Page 29

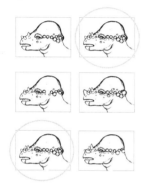

Page 30
Answers will vary.

Page 31

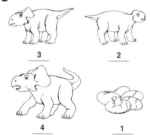

Page 33

This Maiasaura nest was found in (m)(o)(n) t a n a.
The remains of the adult were near a large n (e) s t.
The nest was (r) o u n d in shape.
The t e e t (h) of the baby dinosaurs were worn because they had been eating p l a n t (s).

"Good m o t h e r lizard"

Sample answer: Adults feed, protect, and groom their young. They sometimes build a nest or another kind of home or shelter. They teach the young how to survive on their own.

Page 34

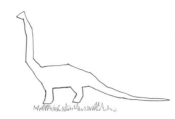

Page 35

Page 36

Page 37
Sample answer: Velociraptor liked to steal eggs from the nests of other dinosaurs and eat them.
Sample answers: rap, trap, tape, voice, price, pace, part, port, ravel, travel, carp, poor, pave, rave, crave, cave, love, cove, pare, pair, act, actor, octave, lace, race, rat, tap, pat, ice, lice, vice, lope, rope, and trip.

Page 38
Parent: Check child's work.

Page 39

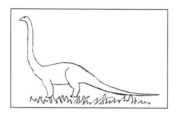

Stegosaurus had a small h e (a) d.
Stegosaurus had sharp s (p) i k e s on the end of its tail.
Stegosaurus was about 25 f e e (t) long.
Stegosaurus weighed over 3 t o n (s).
Stegosaurus had bony p (l) a t e s on its back.
Its head was close to the g r o u (n) d.

Stegosaurus ate p l a n t s.

Page 40

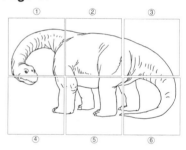

Page 41

Page 42
strong, trees, tough

Page 43

Ankylosaurus weighed f i v e t o n s.
　　　　　　　　　　　1 2 3 4　5 6 7 8

Ankylosaurus had a s h o r t neck.
　　　　　　　　　　8 9 6 10 5

Ankylosaurus had bony plates, s p i k e s, and knobs for armor.
　　　　　　　　　　　　　8 11 2 12 4 8

Ankylosaurus ate p l a n t s.
　　　　　　　　　11 13 14 7 5 8

r e p t i l i a n   t a n k
10 4 11 5 2 13 2 14 7　5 14 7 12

Sample answer: This relative of a reptile has a lot of armor, like an army tank.

Page 44

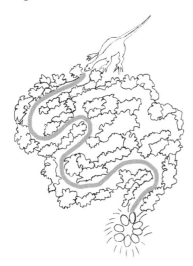

Page 45

Page 46

Page 47

Sample answers: run, sun, ten, tad, sad, rad, ant, rut, cent, tend, send, sent, turn, race, rent, runt, dear, read, tread, stand, canter, trace, traced, rust, rusted, truce, dance, dancer, and trance.
Rest of answers will vary.

Page 48

Yes, Saltosaurus was bigger than a car.
Answers will vary.
Sample answer: An armadillo.

Page 49

Corythosaurus was fairly large in s i z e.

In fact, it was about t h i r t y   f e e t long.

Corythosaurus had a large crest on its h e a d.

Its skin was b u m p y.

It probably ate l e a v e s.

h e l m e t   l i z a r d

Sample Answer: Yes, because the crest on the head of Corythosaurus was like a helmet that protected it.

Page 50

Answers will vary.

Page 51

One is missing an arm, one has more spots, and one has a bigger crest.

Pages 52–53

Answers will vary.

Page 54

Page 55

Pages 56–59

Answers will vary.

Pronunciation Guide

Acrocanthosaurus (ak-roh-CAN-thoh-sor-uss)

Allosaurus (al-oh-SOR-uss)

Ankylosaurus (an-KY-loh-sor-uss)

Apatosaurus (uh-PAT-uh-sor-uss)

Brachiosaurus (BRAK-ee-oh-sor-uss)

Camarasaurus (KAM-ah-ruh-sor-uss)

Camptosaurus (KAMP-tuh-sor-uss)

Coelophysis (seel-oh-FY-siss)

Compsognathus (komp-soh-NAY-thuss)

Corythosaurus (ko-RITH-oh-sor-uss)

Dacentrurus (duh-cen-TROOR-uss)

Deinonychus (dy-NON-ih-kuss)

Dilophosaurus (dy-LOFF-uh-sor-uss)

Diplodocus (dih-PLOD-oh-kuss)

Euoplocephalus (yoo-op-loh-SEF-uh-luss)

Gallimimus (gal-ih-MY-muss)

Hadrosaurus (HAD-roh-sor-uss)

Hylaeosaurus (hi-LEE-oh-sor-uss)

Iguanodon (ee-GWAN-oh-don)

Ingenia (in-GEE-nee-uh)

Maiasaura (my-ee-uh-SOR-uh)

Ornithischians (or-nuh-THISS-kee-unz)

Pachycephalosaurus (pak-ee-SEF-uh-loh-sor-uss)

Paleontologist (pay-lee-uhn-TAHL-uh-jist)

Parasaurolophus (par-uh-sor-ALL-oh-fuss)

Parksosaurus (PARKS-oh-sor-uss)

Pentaceratops (pen-tuh-SAYR-uh-tops)

Plesiosaurus (PLAY-see-oh-sor-uss)

Podokesaurus (poh-DOK-eh-sor-uss)

Protoceratops (proh-toh-SAYR-uh-tops)

Psittacosaurus (SIT-uh-coh-sor-uss)

Pteranodon (tayr-AHN-uh-don)

Saltasaurus (sahl-tuh-SOR-uss)

Saltopus (SALT-oh-puss)

Saurischians (sor-ISS-kee-unz)

Sauropod (SOR-uh-pod)

Stegosaurus (STEG-oh-sor-uss)

Stenonychosaurus (steh-NON-ih-ko-sor-uss)

Styracosaurus (sty-RAK-oh-sor-uss)

Tarbosaurus (TAR-boh-sor-uss)

Triceratops (try-SAYR-uh-tops)

Troödon (TROO-uh-don)

Tyrannosaurus (ty-RAN-oh-sor-uss)

Velociraptor (vuh-LOSS-ih-rap-tor)